Telling the Story of Jesus

Telling the Story of Jesus

Word–Communion–Mission

Cardinal Luis Antonio Tagle

with a foreword by
Cardinal Donald Wuerl

LITURGICAL PRESS
Collegeville, Minnesota

www.litpress.org

Cover design by Stefan Killen Design. Cover photo © Catholic News Service/Tyler Orsburn.

Originally published in Italian as *Raccontare Gesù. Parola–Comunione–Missione* by Luis Antonio Gokim Tagle. © 2014 Editrice Missionaria Italiana, Sermis s.c.r.l., Via di Corticella, 179/4, 40128 Bologna, Italy. www.emi.it.

1	2	3	4	5	6	7	8	9

Library of Congress Control Number: 2014955217

ISBN 978-0-8146-4814-8   978-0-8146-4839-1 (ebook)

Contents

Foreword

The mission the church faces today is widely identified as the New Evangelization. Cardinal Luis Antonio Tagle nicely sums it up as telling the story of Jesus. Saint John Paul II began, many decades ago, to call us to a new period of evangelization. He described it as the announcement of the Good News about Jesus that is "new in ardor, method and expression" (Address to CELAM, March 9, 1983). His successor, Pope Benedict XVI, affirmed that the discernment of "the new demands of evangelization" is a "prophetic" task of the Supreme Pontiff (*Caritas in Veritate* 12). He highlighted that "the entire activity of the church is an expression of love" that seeks to evangelize the world (*Deus Caritas Est* 19).

We see as a hallmark in the papacy of Pope Francis the emphasis that the church "go out" into the world.

When we listen to the pope's talks or read his homilies, we keep hearing over and over words like "go," "invite," "welcome," "embrace," "be there for and with others." We are all brothers and sisters of the same loving Father, he emphasizes, and therefore we are called to care for one another, especially the least among us—those with the most needs.

What Pope Francis invites us to do is focus our attention on the overwhelming blessing that is the love of God in our lives and in our world. When asked to describe himself, he humbly said he was a sinner. So we all are. But he reminded us that we have all been embraced by the love of God.

The invitation of Pope Francis to a fresh way of living the Gospel in our world—which is so desperate for forgiveness, compassion, kindness, and love—is a bright ray of hope as we move forward in the third millennium.

The context of this new emphasis was discussed at the time of the Synod on the New Evangelization and reflected in both the exhortation of Pope Francis and the interventions made during the 2014 Synod on the Pastoral Challenges of the Family in the Context of Evangelization. Secularism best describes the new dominant vision that influences so much of our world.

The Christian way of life and the Gospel vision of right and wrong, virtue, and God's love all seem to be eclipsed by a strong secular voice that comes even from some within the church that find the church's perennial teaching somehow distasteful. So pervasive is this "other message" that today many never even get to hear the truth, richness, and joy of the authentic Gospel of Christ.

The New Evangelization recognizes that in countries where the Gospel has already been preached there is an "eclipse of the sense of God" (*Evangelium Vitae* 21). What brings a new urgency to our mission is the acknowledgment of just how widespread and profound is the new secularism.

It is against this background—a diminished appreciation of the faith—that Pope Francis called all of us to a process of outreach centered on the 2014 synod of bishops and the forthcoming 2015 Synod on the Vocation and Mission of the Family in the Church and the Modern World.

Cardinal Tagle, who serves on the council for the synod, offers a refreshing focus on the New Evangelization with three presentations on the Word of God, the Eucharist, and the mission of the church. He, with his well-recognized ability as a true master catechist, reflects on the core of the kerygma and how we share it.

The Gospel offers us a whole way of seeing life and the world around us. We recognize that we cannot impose this Good News of the gratuitous love of God, but at the same time do need to recognize that we are called to share this message, to bring it to others, to let them know of the beauty of life in Christ.

We bring a fuller vision—offering another dimension to life. In the Sermon on the Mount presented in Matthew's gospel, we hear of a new way of life and how it involves the merciful, those who hunger and thirst for righteousness, those who mourn, the peacemakers, the poor in spirit. Here we learn of the call to be salt of the earth and a light set on a lamp stand.

Later in that same gospel, we hear the extraordinary dictum that we should see in one another the very presence of Christ. Jesus' disciples are challenged to envision a world where not only the hungry are fed, the thirsty are given drink, the stranger is welcomed, and the naked are clothed, but also most amazingly sins are forgiven and eternal life is pledged.

Jesus invites us into God's family. Jesus is the "only Son of God" (John 3:18). We receive our status by adoption. "As proof that you are children, God sent the spirit of his Son into our hearts, crying out, 'Abba, Father!' So you are no longer a slave but a child, and if a child then also an heir, through God" (Gal 4:6-7).

Christian life is defined by an encounter with Jesus. Our proclamation is focused on Jesus, his Gospel and his way. When Jesus first came among us, he offered a whole new way of living. The excitement spread as God's Son, who is also one of us, announced the coming of the kingdom. The invitation to discipleship and a place in the kingdom that he held out to those who heard him, he continues to offer today. This has been true for twenty centuries.

Already in just one generation after the resurrection of Jesus, St. Paul could write to the Corinthians that he was passing on to them "what I also received: that Christ died for our sins in accordance with the scriptures; that he was buried; that he was raised on the third day in accordance with the scriptures" (1 Cor 15:3-4). Paul is calling the attention of the church to the living tradition passed on from those who saw the risen Lord. He is speaking of an established, verifiable tradition within the lifetime of people who could vouch for what they had seen and what they had preached. We are dealing with a real person, and there is continuity between the person who was taken down from the cross, wrapped in the shroud, and placed in the tomb and the one who is now risen from the dead and who appeared to numerous people.

For his readers, Cardinal Tagle highlights the primordial significance of the Word of God. His first chapter is titled "Communion in the Word through Mary." Together with the second section, "The Eucharist, the Life of Christ in Our Lives," he engages the issue of how and where we encounter Jesus—if we are to be his followers, his missionary disciples.

Following his reflections on the importance of the Word of God and the central role of the Eucharist, Cardinal Tagle challenges his readers to the mission of "Telling the Story of Jesus." The disciple—in the words of Pope Francis—must be a missionary disciple.

In response to the question, How do we come to know and encounter Jesus today? we look to the church. The answer is found in the only living witness to the Lord Jesus, the only witness who can say, I was there when Jesus died, when he rose, when he ascended into heaven, and when he sent the gift of the Holy Spirit. That one remaining living witness is Christ's body, his church. It is in living continuity with that church that you and I find our connectedness to the gospels and to Christ himself.

Pope Francis begins his apostolic exhortation, *Evangelii Gaudium*, with the reminder that "the joy of the Gospel fills the hearts and lives of all who encounter Jesus. . . . With Christ joy is constantly born again" (1). Our message should be one that inspires others to joyfully follow us along the path to the kingdom of God. Joy must characterize the evangelizer. Ours is a message of great rejoicing; Christ is risen, Christ is with us. Whatever our circumstances, our witness should radiate with the fruits of the Holy Spirit including love, peace, and joy (cf. Gal 5:22).

This is a time of new Pentecost for the church. Our goal is to participate in that Pentecostal outpouring of God's grace and love by providing people with an understanding of the faith so that they are well equipped to live out their lives as witnesses to Christ and the Gospel.

Cardinal Tagle's reflections, presented by Liturgical Press under the title of *Telling the Story of Jesus*, are a joyful invitation to do just that—renewed with a deeper appreciation of the importance of the Word of God, the Eucharist, the church, and our part, now, as bearers of the Good News.

Cardinal Donald Wuerl
Archbishop of Washington

Communion in the Word through Mary

The 50th International Eucharistic Congress has been providing us with a wealth of reflection on "The Eucharist: Communion with Christ and with One Another." Having explored communion in baptism, in marriage and family, in the priestly ministry, in reconciliation, and in suffering and healing, we now turn to communion in the Word through Mary. Allow me to develop this fascinating theme in two parts. In the first section I will dwell on communion in the Word of God, and in the second I will meditate on Mary's experience of communion in the Word as a model for the church.

Communion in the Word of God

How will we approach this topic? It might help to turn to ordinary human experience. One common way of establishing a connection with another human being is through conversation or dialogue. This occurs so often that we seldom notice its significance. Take a person who sees a good movie and excitedly shares it with a friend, who in turn goes to the cinema to watch it due to the friend's satisfying experience. Then they spend hours talking about the film, digressing many times to the stories of their lives. Or take another person whose marriage is falling apart and calls up a friend, who becomes equally distressed after listening intently. Then they spend hours talking about the sorrows of life, finding hope in each other's presence. We now see that human communion ordinarily happens when someone begins to tell a story to another person who listens, enters the experience, and makes it one's own. In the exchange that follows, their roles shift and alternate: the one who narrates also listens, the one who listens spontaneously narrates. Two persons and their unique worlds meet in a unity that goes beyond them.

This simple process called communion in the word is at the heart of the mystery and mission of the church. Saint John vividly portrays it in his first letter (1:1-4):

What was from the beginning,
>   what we have heard,
>   what we have seen with our eyes,
>   what we looked upon
>   and touched with our hands
>   concerns the Word of life—
for the life was made visible;
>   we have seen it and testify to it
>   and proclaim to you the eternal life
>   that was with the Father and was made visible to
>   us—
what we have seen and heard
>   we proclaim now to you,
>   so that you too may have [communion] with us;
>   for our [communion] is with the Father
>   and with his Son, Jesus Christ.
We are writing this so that our joy may be complete.

Human communion. What St. John is describing is similar to the ordinary experiences of communion between two or more human beings we mentioned earlier. But St. John's account involves a special person, called an apostle, who proclaims a special word to a listener. Their conversation blossoms into communion with each other, which in reality is their communion with the Father and with Jesus Christ, the Word made visible in the flesh. What a great mystery unfolding in a quite ordinary human experience! Let us delve deeper into this beautiful text.

What word does the apostle share with his listener? It is the Word of Life, present with the Father and made visible. The word that the apostle proclaims is Jesus Christ, the Word made flesh. Simply put, the apostle's word is Jesus Christ. We can see it plainly in the New Testament. After Pentecost, Peter proclaimed to his hearers the person of Jesus the Nazorean sent by God, crucified, but whom God raised from the dead, making him Lord and Messiah (Acts 2:22-24, 36). Peter declared that salvation comes to us in the name of Jesus (Acts 4:12). But let us not forget that Peter was able to proclaim Jesus because he had heard, seen, and touched Jesus.

Another great apostle, Paul, tirelessly spoke of nothing but Jesus Christ. Not being a member of the Twelve, he nevertheless was graced by a special revelation from the risen Lord that changed his life radically (Acts 9:1-19). But he received his knowledge about the earthly life and ministry of Jesus from others who had spoken to him about Jesus. In 1 Corinthians, he said, "For I handed on to you as of first importance what I also received" (15:3). His encounter with the living Lord and the story of Jesus transmitted to him have equipped him to proclaim him as the Messiah and Lord.

In a nutshell, the apostle proclaims the person of Jesus Christ, the story of his ministry, preaching, and healing centered on the reign of God. He narrates how people rejected and crucified him and how God raised him from death. At his resurrection, Jesus was revealed as the Anointed One of God, indeed, the divine Son of God who exercises full dominion over the world and its future. Whether it is Peter, Paul, Stephen, Philip, or Mary of Magdala, the joyful story told is that of Jesus Christ and the destiny of the world in him who is divine Savior and Messiah.

We must note that the apostle renders an objective account concerning Jesus. But he can hand on facts about Jesus because he has experienced him personally. He has heard, seen, looked upon, and touched Jesus. Thus an apostle's familiarity with Jesus enables him to be the source of a historical proclamation about him. Here the objective and the subjective, the factual and the personal, meet. Those who have listened to Jesus can tell this story to others in a credible way. Then their listeners accept Jesus into their dreams, joys, pains, hopes, frustrations, questions, and wisdoms. They bring all these that comprise their worlds as they listen toward communion.

You might say, "Well and good for the original companions of Jesus. They saw him firsthand. But how can we who are separated from Jesus by centuries talk meaningfully about him?" Let us not forget that Jesus is alive. He is truly raised from the dead! He is with us now. He rules the world. He continues to visit the homes of many Marthas and Marys of our time to enjoy a restful meal. He continues to weep at our tombs the way he did at the tomb of Lazarus his friend. He continues to quietly call on the Zacchaeuses of our age to pay back what they have stolen. He continues to have compassion for widows who carry their children to the grave. He continues to see the hungry crowds and asks us to feed them with our five loaves and two fish. He continues to welcome the weary and heavy-burdened to find rest in him. He continues to cry out to God with the suffering victims, "My God, my God, why have you forsaken me?" My brothers and sisters, please do not say we have not seen, heard, looked upon, and touched Jesus. Yes, we have. If only we could listen to him more attentively, we will have stories of Jesus to tell.

Communion with Christ and the Father. Saint John claims that the human communion between the messenger and listener centered on the Word of life is not merely a human transaction. It is at the same time their communion with Jesus Christ and with the Father. In other words, this quite ordinary human togetherness has a transcendent dimension.

We already said that the word proclaimed by the apostle is not only a historical fact that could be verified by scientific methods but also an experience of the mystery of the Word of God made flesh, who now lives eternally with the Father. Where two or three are in communion with each other on account of Jesus, he is in their midst. This is not just a sociological fact. We believe that this communion with Christ is the action of the Holy Spirit, who teaches and reminds us of all that Jesus taught (John 14:26). The same Holy Spirit enables us to confess, "Jesus is Lord" (1 Cor 12:3). The Spirit "assimilates" us with Jesus Christ so that as children in the Son we can also cry out, "Abba, Father!" (Rom 8:14-15). Now it is clear that communion with Jesus in the Holy Spirit brings about communion with the Father. Jesus reveals the Father to us so that whoever sees him sees the Father also (John 8:9). As the Way (John 14:6), Jesus gives us access to the Father (Eph 2:18) and to the Father's house, where he prepares a place for us (John 14:2-3).

What a marvelous communion in the Word that gives us weak and sinful human beings a participation in the eternal communion of the Father, Son, and Holy Spirit! This is the mystery of the church celebrated in the Eucharist, where the Word proclaimed and received is the same Word become flesh eaten as the Bread of Life. Communion in the Word, experienced at every Eucharist, is one contribution of the church to the building up of a world of unity and peace.

We see in our time so much exchange of words happening at high speed and across international boundaries. But unfortunately the world is as divided as ever. Why is communion not achieved in spite of the exchange of words? Because Jesus is not the word they share and receive. When financial wizards talk about ways of manipulating the economy for their own profit, you do not call that communion; that is corruption! When politicians talk to people about grand promises without intending to fulfill them, you do not call that communion; that is cheating! When the powerful "negotiate" among themselves while neglecting the weak, you do not call that communion; that is oppression! When so-called enterprising persons deal with each other on how women and children could be profitable merchandise, you do not call that communion; that is slavery! When communion consists in Jesus, who is the Word of life, then the common good becomes central. And that is pleasing to God's eyes.

To close this section, let me tell you a story. On my way back to the Philippines from one of my trips to Rome, I had a layover of more than three hours in an airport. To while away the time, I went around looking for a coffee bar. I found one, placed my order, and paid. This is a normal human transaction, so I thought. The man who handed me the coffee and the receipt asked, "Are you a priest?" A bit surprised, I said, "Yes." Then the next question, "Are you a Filipino?" Now truly amused, I smiled and said, "Yes." He turned to one corner of the store and, while waving to some people hidden from my sight, said, "He is the one! Come!" A group of Filipinos working in that airport came rushing to me. They said that they followed on YouTube or Facebook my weekly reflections on the readings for Sunday Mass shown on television, titled *The Word Exposed*. Due to their irregular work schedules, they could not always be present at Mass. Through the Word they experience some form of communion with Jesus, they said. One woman commented, "Through your stories, we feel united with our families back home. How we miss them!" Communion in the Word can happen online and in unexpected places. We shared our stories until my coffee turned cold.

Communion in the Word through Mary

The Blessed Virgin Mary experienced communion in the Word in an utterly unique way. As a listener to and the bearer of the Word made flesh, she is the model and teacher for the church. Let us contemplate her immaculate heart, where she guarded and pondered the mystery of the Word.

In her journey of faith, Mary initially received proclamations about Jesus, the Word of God who will become her son in the flesh. God sent messengers or "apostles" to her. From them she heard about her Son.

1. In the annunciation (Luke 1:26-38), the angel Gabriel sent by God proclaims a word to Mary. The very greeting "Hail!" signals that a special moment is about to happen to Mary and her people Israel that awaits the promised Messiah. Gabriel tells Mary that she will bear a son. But who is this child? In the words of the angel, Mary learns that her son will be great, for he is the Son of the Most High, the Son of

David who will rule forever. This child will be holy, the Son of God. She who is a virgin will conceive by the overshadowing of the Holy Spirit. His name shall be Jesus, for God saves.

The angel proclaims to Mary a word about the Son of God. She listens intelligently, accepts in faith, and utters her word, "Behold, I am the handmaid of the Lord. May it be done to me according to your word"! This is a singular moment of communion between God and Mary. By calling herself the handmaid of the Lord, she does not debase herself but accepts the grace of being part of God's saving action. She speaks in union with her people Israel in welcoming the Messiah that they have been pining for. Mary becomes daughter Zion, the ark of the new covenant, by her communion with God in the Word.

By being in communion with the Word, the church, like Mary, will actively promote God's saving plan in the world—not advancing its own projects but the will of God.

2. Let us now follow Mary as she visits her kinswoman Elizabeth, who is known to be barren but is now with child (Luke 1:39-56). Filled with the Holy Spirit, Elizabeth tells Mary that the fruit of her womb

is the Lord. She is the bearer of the Lord! As David danced before the ark of the covenant, now the baby in Elizabeth's womb dances before the ark of the new covenant.

Mary listens, accepts, and utters her word, a song in praise of the merciful God, the immortal *Magnificat*. She sings of God's mercy in her life and, through her, in the life of the poor and the oppressed of Israel. In her prayer she gives voice again to Sarah, Leah, and Judith. In her song we hear Miriam, Deborah, and Hannah singing once more. Accepting the revelation about her son through Elizabeth, Mary becomes the mother of grace and hope for the poor.

By being in communion with the Word, the church, like Mary, will be the companion of the poor so that they can recover their voice and sing for joy.

3. Then the time for Mary to give birth to her Son comes (Luke 2:1-20). They are in Bethlehem, the city of David. The Son of the Most High God is born in a manger. God sends messengers to tell Mary about her Son; they are the lowly shepherds. An angel that appeared to them at their night watch said that a Savior who is Messiah and Lord was born in Bethlehem. This birth would be news of joy to all the people. Indeed a

multitude of heavenly host appeared to them in joyful praise of God.

Mary, with Joseph by her side, listens, accepts, and responds in silence. What mother would not be rendered speechless by such a report about her son? Amazed like the rest who hear the story of the shepherds, she keeps all these things, "reflecting on them in her heart." The most meaningful word is uttered in silence. Gazing upon the baby wrapped in swaddling clothes, she nurtures her communion in the Word through silence.

By being in communion with the Word, the church, like Mary, will gladly listen to the lowly and the poor with reverential silence, listening to God speaking through them.

4. With Mary's ritual purification over, it is now time to present the Child Jesus in the temple (Luke 2:22-38). God sends another poor man to utter a word about Jesus to Mary and Joseph—Simeon, filled with the Holy Spirit. With him is Anna, a poor widow. Like the many poor people of Israel, they search for freedom and joy in the promised Messiah. They recognize the Child. Simeon tells his parents that he is salvation (his name is Jesus), "a light for revelation to the Gentiles"

and glory for Israel. In this Child the nations of the world and Israel will be gathered in communion. But he will also be a sign to be contradicted, destined for the fall and rise of many in Israel.

Mary and Joseph are amazed at these words. She comes to the temple to offer to God no less than what God has given her, namely, God's Son who is her son. But the news of joy from Simeon is coupled with the disturbing word of contradiction that will not spare Mary, for she will be pierced by a sword. What is this sword? It is the Word of God, "living and effective, sharper than any two-edged sword, penetrating even between soul and spirit" (Heb 4:12). The sword is Jesus, the Word of God. She is the mother of the One who will bear the cross. Mary listens, accepts, and responds in amazement. She goes home to Nazareth, where the Child grows in wisdom and grace. She nurtures Jesus her son, who will bring her both joy and sorrow.

By being in communion with the Word, the church, like Mary, will proclaim Jesus in season or out of season, whether accepted or rejected, joyful with him, sorrowful with him (2 Tim 4:2).

At this point, a shift occurs. From now on, the messenger who will speak to Mary about Jesus is Jesus himself.

5. The scene is the annual Passover feast. The family joins many pilgrims to Jerusalem. The boy Jesus is twelve years old (Luke 2:41-52). After completing their duties in the festivities and offering sacrifice, Mary and Joseph return to Nazareth but Jesus stays behind, unbeknownst to them. After three days of searching, they find him in the temple, listening to the teachers and asking them questions. Mary asks the boy why he did this to her and his father, to which he responds, "Why were you looking for me? Did you not know that I must be in my Father's house?" The Mother now listens to the stunning word of her Son. "Who is this boy?" she must be asking. Maybe thoughts like these cross her mind: Sitting with the teachers in his Father's house, Jesus will surely fulfill the Law and the Prophets. Seeing the blood of the animals offered in his Father's house, he knows that the sacrifice of a pure heart is more pleasing to the Father than burnt offerings of animals.

Mary listens and accepts Jesus' enigmatic word to her, even if she does not understand. As before, she keeps all these things in her heart. In that immaculate heart overflowing with faith she knows that one day her Son will disappear again. She knows that her heart will be pierced when that day comes. She knows that she will see him again after three days. She knows her heart will rejoice on that blessed third day.

By being in communion with the Word, the church, like Mary, will look for Jesus among the lost, wounded, tired, and abandoned and lead them with rejoicing to the Father's house.

6. Let us now turn to the public ministry of Jesus. The wedding at Cana is the site of his first "sign" (John 2:1-12). Mary tells Jesus that they have run short of wine. He utters a word to his mother that unsettles us: "Woman, how does your concern affect me? My hour has not yet come." For Jesus, his hour is the moment of glorification on the cross, when life that is given up produces much fruit unto eternity (John 12:23-26). Maybe out of lack of understanding or out of helplessness, Mary listens, accepts, and utters her own words to the servers: "Do whatever he tells you." They obey her and Jesus. And the miracle happens. It is the beginning of Jesus' hour after all. The wine is God's word and wisdom that will flow in abundance at the coming of the Messiah. Mary, who is obedient to her Son's word, now asks the servers to give Jesus full obedience as well. In the communion of obedience to the word, miracles happen.

We run out of wine too: the wine of wisdom, understanding, insight, energy, and meaning. God seems to be unreachable at times. When those moments come, know that Mary is close by. She sees our empty jars. She approaches Jesus for us. If we listen to Jesus and do what he tells us, those jars will overflow with unbelievably good wine.

By being in communion with the Word, the church, like Mary, will be attentive to the emptiness experienced by our age and lead people not to us but to Jesus, for he alone can make miracles happen through his word.

7. According to the gospels, the last time Jesus talks to Mary is before he breathes his last on the cross (John 19:23-28). Jewish thought teaches that death disrupts communion, but not so for Jesus.

On this hour of his glorification, with the four pagan soldiers vying for his tunic, and the four women and the Beloved Disciple mourning at the foot of his cross, he tells his mother, "Woman, behold, your son." Then he says to the disciple, "Behold, your mother." Jesus reveals and creates his mother as the mother of the new family of disciples, of "those who hear the word of God and act on it" (Luke 8:21). Jesus' death, freely embraced in communion with God and with sinners, does not destroy community but gives birth to a new family. By the word of Jesus, Mary becomes the mother of both his disciples and the people called to believe in him. She responds to Jesus by doing what he says—she goes to the home of the Beloved Disciple.

Even now Jesus beholds mothers and fathers who lose their children to hunger, diseases, wars, illegal drugs, sex tourism, immorality, false philosophies, and empty utopias. Jesus tells us to take care of the sorrowful mothers and fathers, for they are our parents too. He tells us to look after the lost children of the world, for they are our daughters and sons too. No wound is so great that it could not be healed by love.

By being in communion with the Word, the church, like Mary, will be the seed of the new family of justice, healing, and peace.

I recall a dark day when I was still a priest serving in my home diocese. One morning a young priest, thirty-two years of age, was found dead. His body, stabbed thirty-two times, was left in a rice field. He was a former student of mine. At the wake I walked his mother toward the coffin. Upon seeing her lifeless son, she shed tears of sorrow and cried out in prayer, "My God, you know how heavy my heart was when my son entered the seminary. But you prevailed. So I surrendered him to you. Now you took him again from me. If it is your wish, then I give him totally to you. He is all yours." I could not believe what I was hearing. A few days later, in a forum on justice that we attended, someone asked her, "What would you do if the killer of your son is presented to you?" I thought it was an insensitive question, but before I could stop her, she already responded, "Dear police, do not hesitate to bring my son's killer to me. Do not fear. I will not hurt him. I just want to know why he did it. I will observe the dictates of justice but deep in my heart, I will forgive, for Jesus tells me to forgive. My love might help make the killer a better person." Once again, I could not believe what was happening. But I know we were again at the foot of the cross and hearing the same words, "Woman, behold, your son. Son, behold, your mother." Those days were followed by many more weeks of listening to the stories of the priest's mother about her son and her family, stories that I would hear for the first time. I could not help but think then that I have come to know the priest much better now that he is gone but made more vividly present by his mother's stories.

8. I believe this also happened to Mary and her new family. After Jesus' ascension into heaven, the extended family of disciples with Mary went to the Upper Room to await the promised Holy Spirit, who would remind us about Jesus (Acts 1:13-14). I would like to think that with the help of the same Spirit that overshadowed her at the annunciation, Mary could now understand better the things about Jesus that she had kept in her heart. Now she could proclaim her stories to her new sons and daughters: what she has heard, seen with her eyes, looked upon, and touched with her hands concerning her Son, the Word of life. She must have ended every story by saying, "Do whatever he tells you." Like Mary, go and tell the good news of Jesus to the ends of the earth. And do whatever he tells you. Amen.

—delivered on June 16, 2012, at the 50th International Eucharistic Congress in Dublin, Ireland

The Eucharist, the Life of Christ in Our Lives

Spiritual Worship and Authentic Adoration

We have come to the part of the Congress devoted to a reflection on "The Eucharist, the Life of Christ in Our Lives." These past days we have been affirming that the church lives by the gift of the life of Christ. This essential part of our faith is experienced in a unique and special way in the Eucharist, where the church receives again and again the life of Christ to become its very own life. What a wonderful mystery it is to live by the life of Christ. Jesus' mission is to give his life so that others may live. In John 6:51 he says, "I am the living bread that came down from heaven. Whoever eats of this bread will live forever; and the bread that I will give for the life of the world is my flesh." Jesus the Bread of Life is a gift from the Father. Those who eat this bread, who receive Jesus into their persons, will have life. He will lay down his life, so that others "may have life, and have it abundantly" (John 10:10). Every Eucharist proclaims, "God so loved the world that he gave his only Son, so that everyone who believes in him may not perish but may have eternal life" (John 3:16). Because the life of Christ is oriented toward others, the church must share this life with the world. The life of Christ is his gift to the church that is meant to be the church's gift to the world.

In the Eucharist we don't only receive the life of Christ. Beholding this most precious gift, we are moved as well to worship and adore the triune God. The Eucharist does not fail to evoke from grateful hearts the worship and adoration that God deserves. But as we worship and adore we realize that it is Jesus who guides us on the way of true worship and adoration. We will dwell on these two elements of living the Eucharist: spiritual worship and authentic adoration. But first let us describe the sacrifice of Jesus Christ.

The Sacrifice of Jesus Christ

The Catholic tradition refers to the Eucharist as the sacrament of Jesus' sacrifice. In the Judaic tradition, the offering of ritual sacrifices occupied a central place in the worship of God's people. Was the sacrifice of Jesus no different from other temple sacrifices like the pouring of the blood of animals and the burning of offerings? What made up the sacrificial worship of Jesus? It is time to consider the unique worship of Jesus contained in his unique sacrifice. For this we turn to the letter to the Hebrews. In Hebrews 7:27 it is stated, "Unlike the other high priests, he has no need to offer sacrifices day after day, first for his own sins, and then for those of the people; this he did once for all when he offered himself." He offered himself! "He entered once for all into the Holy Place, not with the blood of goats and calves, but with his own blood, thus obtaining eternal redemption" (Heb 9:12). Jesus offered his blood, his very life and not any animal substitute. The letter further says, "It is by God's will that we have been sanctified through the offering of the body of Jesus Christ once for all" (Heb 10:10). The sacrificial worship of Jesus Christ, therefore, consists in the offering of his body, his blood, and his life. The apex of this sacrifice of self-oblation occurs on the cross and reaches its completion in the heavenly sanctuary or in Jesus' glorification. We have gone beyond mere ritual sacrifice to the living sacrifice of self-giving. Jesus' worship culminates in the surrender of his humanity and its entry into God's presence for the sake of the world.

At this point we draw our attention to the question of how the self-offering of Jesus becomes true sacrifice and worship. We know many people who offer themselves to something or someone, such as parents, teachers, public servants, or even hardened criminals. Does every self-offering qualify as a sacrificial worship? So we ask, how does Jesus' offering of his body and blood acquire the quality of genuine sacrifice? The letter to the Hebrews gives two elements of Jesus' self-oblation.

First, we hear in Hebrews 5:7-8, "In the days of his flesh, Jesus offered up prayers and supplications, with loud cries and tears, to the one who was able to save him from death, and he was heard because of his reverent submission. Although he was a Son, he learned obedience through what he suffered." This is the first aspect that makes his self-offering an act of worship, namely, his obedience or reverent submission to the Father who willed that people be saved and brought to glory (Heb 2:10). Self-offering motivated by the desire to prove oneself, to achieve success, or to promote self-interest falls short of being a moment of worship. Jesus' sacrifice of his life was not focused on himself or his agenda but rather was a response to the Father who had sent him. The fulfillment of his saving will pleases the Father more than any burnt sacrifices (Heb 8:9). Thus obedience to God makes the gift of self an act of worship.

Second, his worship includes his solidarity with feeble sinners. In Hebrews 4:15-16 it is stated, "For we do not have a high priest who is unable to sympathize with our weaknesses, but we have one who in every respect has been tested as we are, yet without sin. Let us therefore approach the throne of grace with boldness, so that we may receive mercy and find grace in time of need." His oneness with weak humanity was essential to his priestly service or worship on behalf of the people. Hebrews 2:17-18 states eloquently, "Therefore he had to become like his brothers and sisters in every respect, so that he might be a merciful and faithful high priest in the service of God, to make a sacrifice of atonement for the sins of the people. Because he himself was tested by what he suffered, he is able to help those who are being tested." Here the image of priestly service or worship is applied to the redemptive mission of Jesus. His embrace of the trials and sufferings of human beings has made him a brother who can now truly intercede for them before the Father's mercy rather than judge them harshly. He worships through supplications to God welling up from his compassion for erring sinners. In other words, Jesus' prayer to the Father gives voice to humankind's laments and hopes that he has made his own.

In summary, we can say that the worship of Jesus is the sacrifice of his own life offered to fulfill the Father's will to save sinners, whose weaknesses he shares in order to lift them to the mercy of God as a compassionate High Priest and brother. Obedience to God and compassionate action on behalf of sinners form one unitary act of worship. They cannot be separated from each other. Jesus' intercessory life for weak humanity before God is his priestly worship that fulfills God's will. Ultimately, we see in Jesus' worship the embodiment of loving God with one's whole being and loving one's neighbors as oneself. Every time we come to the Eucharist, Jesus renews his unique sacrifice and invites us to share in his worship of self-oblation.

The Spiritual Worship of the Baptized

In baptism, we begin sharing in Jesus' sacrifice of obedience to the Father in solidarity with sinners. Baptism unites us to Jesus' sacrificial death and newness of life. Saint Paul tells us in Romans 6:3-4, "Do you not know that all of us who have been baptized into Christ Jesus were baptized into his death? Therefore we have been buried with him by baptism into death, so that, just as Christ was raised from the dead by the glory of the Father, so we too might walk in newness of life." In union with Christ and in the power of the Holy Spirit, we are enabled to offer our life for God; that involves dying to sin. Renunciation of sin and faith in God form the fundamental worship and sacrifice of the baptized, made possible by our sharing in the sacrifice of Jesus. In this light we can understand Saint Paul's words in Romans 12:1: "I appeal to you therefore, brothers and sisters, by the mercies of God, to present your bodies as a living sacrifice, holy and acceptable to God, which is your spiritual worship." Like Jesus we are to offer a living sacrifice not made up of calves, goats, and grain but of lives dedicated to God. This living sacrifice united with Christ's sacrifice builds up the Christian community as well. First Peter rightly states, "Come to him, a living stone, though rejected by mortals yet chosen and precious in God's sight, and like living stones, let yourselves be built into a spiritual house, to be a holy priesthood, to offer spiritual sacrifices acceptable to God though Jesus Christ" (2:4-5).

It is evident that the living sacrifice of the baptized includes ethical demands. Saint Paul tells us that offering our bodies as a living sacrifice will happen only if we are not "conformed to this world" but are "transformed by the renewing of [our] minds, so that [we] may discern what is the will of God—what is good and acceptable and perfect" (Rom 12:2). Conformity to the will of God is a key to the sacrifice of one's life. It also involves living in genuine love, contributing to the needs of others, "rejoic[ing] with those who rejoice, weep[ing] with those who weep" (Rom 12:9-15). We are back where we started. Jesus' sacrifice of obedience to the Father and communion with weak sinners is the same sacrifice that the baptized are asked to offer as a gift to the world. This is so because we have received his life in baptism. And in every eucharistic memorial of Christ's sacrifice, we are taken up into its life-giving power so that we can share it for the life of the world.

It is ironic that during the public ministry of Jesus, he was not always perceived as someone who offered a sacrifice pleasing to God. Instead of being praised for being obedient, he was frequently accused of transgressing the law of God. No wonder, some people attributed his miracles to the power of the prince of demons rather than to divine intervention. His critics even took his repeated claims of oneness with God as blasphemy rather than as revelation of God's truth. They concluded that God was as displeased with him as they were. He was dangerous for the nation and the temple. For indeed Jesus' sacrifice of obedience took on a seemingly disobedient or irreverent expression.

It is interesting to note that quite often, Jesus was denounced as a violator of God's law when he showed compassion for the weak, the poor, the sick, women, and public sinners. He offered new life to those considered impure by eating and mingling with them. He assured them that God was not distant and there was hope in God's loving mercy. But he himself got no mercy from his adversaries, only ridicule for disobeying laws that were supposed to embody God's will. Jesus suffered on account of his self-offering for those loved by God. But he never wavered in his sacrifice. In the process he exposed the false gods that people worshiped, erroneous notions of holiness, and the blindness of righteous people to the visitations of God. Jesus' sacrifice uncovered the link between the worship of false gods and insensitivity to the needy. An idolater easily loses compassion for the weak. Though he was judged, Jesus was the one actually judging the untrue worship that kept people blind and deaf to the true God and the poor.

The church that lives the life of Christ and offers his living sacrifice cannot run away from its mission to unearth the false gods worshiped by the world. How many people have exchanged the true God for idols like profit, prestige, pleasure, and control? Those who worship false gods also dedicate their lives to them. In reality these false gods are self-interests. To keep these false gods, their worshipers sacrifice other people's lives and the earth. It is sad that those who worship idols sacrifice other people while preserving themselves and their interests. How many factory workers are being denied just wages for the god of profit? How many women are being sacrificed to the god of domination? How many children are being sacrificed to the god of lust? How many trees, rivers, hills are being sacrificed to the god of "progress"? How many poor people are being sacrificed to the god of greed? How many defenseless people are being sacrificed to the god of national security?

The church, however, must also constantly examine its fidelity to Jesus' sacrifice of obedience to God and compassion for the poor. Like those who opposed Jesus in the name of authentic religion, we could be blind to God and neighbors because of self-righteousness, spiritual pride, and rigidity of mind. Ecclesiastical customs and persons, when naively and narrowly deified and glorified, might become hindrances to true worship and compassion. I am disturbed when some people who do not even know me personally conclude that my being a bishop automatically makes me closer to God than they could ever be. My words are God's words, my desires are God's, my anger is God's, and my actions are God's. If I am not cautious, I might just believe it and start demanding the offerings of the best food and wine, money, car, house, adulation, and submission. After all, I am "God"! I might take so much delight in my stature and its benefits that I might end up being callous to the needs of the poor and the earth.

I remember an experience in the market of our town of Imus, the seat of our diocese. One Saturday morning I went to monitor the prices of goods and the condition of the simple market vendors. I saw a woman selling fruit and vegetables in a corner. She was one of those who went to Sunday Mass regularly. It was only ten o'clock in the morning but she was already closing her store. So I asked her the reason. She told me, "I belong to a prayer group. We have a big assembly this afternoon. Some tasks were assigned to me. So I want to be there early." Upon hearing this, the pragmatic side of me surfaced. I responded, "The Lord will understand if you extend your working hours. You have a family to support. You can benefit from additional income. I am sure the Lord will understand." With a smile, she said, "But bishop, the Lord has been faithful to me. The Lord has always been there for us. We may not be rich but we have enough to live by. Why will I fear?" Then looking at me tenderly, she said, "Are you not a bishop? Are you not supposed to be encouraging me in faith?" I was quite embarrassed. But for me it was an experience of spiritual worship. I, the religiously and culturally accepted presence of God, was revealed to be a faltering representation of God. That simple woman, offering herself to God in trust for love of her family, became for me the manifestation of the presence of

God. She had brought the eucharistic sacrifice and Jesus' spiritual worship from the elegant cathedral to the noise and dirt of the marketplace. God must have been well pleased.

Authentic Adoration

This leads me to the final part of my conference. Let us briefly reflect on adoration. Worship is so intimately related to adoration that they could be considered as one. The sacrifice or spiritual worship of Jesus on the cross is his supreme act of adoration. In the Eucharist, the church joins Jesus in adoring the God of life. But the practice of eucharistic adoration enlivens some features of worship.

We believe that the presence of Christ in the Eucharist continues beyond the liturgy. At any time we can adore the Blessed Sacrament and join the Lord's self-offering to God for the life of the world. Adoration connotes being present, resting, and beholding. In adoration, we are present to Jesus whose sacrifice is ever present to us. Abiding in him, we are assimilated more deeply into his self-giving. Beholding Jesus, we receive and are transformed by the mystery we adore. Eucharistic adoration is similar to standing at the foot of the cross of Jesus, being a witness to his sacrifice of life and being renewed by it.

Aside from the Blessed Mother and the Beloved Disciple who kept vigil with the dying Jesus, the Roman centurion who had been watching over Jesus when he died could also be a model of adoration. Probably the centurion guarded Jesus from his arrest to his death. Seeing Jesus betrayed, arrested, accused, humiliated, stripped, and brutally nailed to the cross, he surprisingly concluded, "This man [is] innocent" (Luke 23:47), and "Truly this man [is] God's Son!" (Matt 27:54; Mark 15:39). Already hardened by many crucifixions he had supervised, he must have seen something new in Jesus. At the conclusion of a routine execution came a profession of faith in Jesus. It was not just another crucifixion after all. It was the manifestation of innocence and of the Son of God. We learn from the centurion's "adoration" that Jesus' sacrifice of life cannot be appreciated for what it truly is unless the horror of the cross is confronted.

Mark's gospel says the centurion stood facing Jesus. Like any leader of guards, he kept careful watch over this criminal Jesus. He did nothing but look at Jesus. Physical nearness was not enough, however. He had to be intent, vigilant, and observant so that he could account for every detail. We learn from the centurion to face Jesus, to keep watch over him, to behold him, to contemplate him. At first the centurion spent hours watching over Jesus out of duty but ended up contemplating him in truth.

What did the centurion see? We can assume that he saw the horror of suffering that preceded Jesus' death. He was an eyewitness to the torment, humiliation, and loneliness inflicted on Jesus when friends betrayed and left him. He must have been shocked to see Judas planting a seemingly caressing kiss that was in fact an act of treachery. He probably wondered how swiftly a band of friends could abandon their teacher to preserve their lives. He heard the lies fabricated in the Sanhedrin and Pilate's surrender to the crowd, despite the lack of a case against Jesus. He beheld people ridiculing Jesus, spitting on him, stripping him, and crucifying him. He heard the painful cry, "My God, my God, why have you forsaken me?" (Mark 15:34). The centurion saw incredible cruelty from friends, leaders, and even a distant God. Betrayal, inhumanity, and viciousness continue up to our time in the many crucifixions of the poor and of creation. We cannot help but wonder why friends, leaders, and God are unresponsive.

But I also believe that in Jesus the centurion saw incredible love, love for the God who had failed to remove this cup of suffering from him, and love for neighbors. For his enemies, he begged the Father's forgiveness (Luke 23:34). To a bandit, he promised paradise (Luke 23:43). For his mother, he secured a new family (John 19:26-27). And to the God who had abandoned him, he abandoned himself: "Father, into your hands I commend my spirit" (Luke 23:46). The centurion saw love blooming in the aridity of inhumanity. Amidst the noise of ridicule and lies, this man Jesus uttered words of fidelity and truth. Everywhere people were shouting "no" to Jesus, but the centurion heard from Jesus only "yes" to the Father, "yes" to neighbors, "yes" to mission. In this horrible cross of hatred and violence, the centurion found love, unwavering love, a love that refused to die, a love that was strong as steel against evil, yet tender before the beloved. Jesus remained faithful to his mission. Thus his death was transformed into life.

When we adore the triune God in praise of the sacrifice of Jesus, we are called to cry for the victims of the indifference of sinful humanity and the helplessness of God. But we also cry in gratitude for the hopeful unfolding of pure love in a broken world. The cross, where the guilt of criminals was sealed, confirmed the innocence of Jesus, the true worshiper of God. His sacrificial worship was his untarnished love of God and profound compassion for sinners. Jesus, who survived such horror with hope and conquered such evil with tenderness and love, was not only innocent. He also showed that he came from above. The centurion believed that Jesus could have come only from God, his Father.

I visited a poor section of a parish that opened a feeding program for malnourished children. The parents were required to supervise the meal of their children. As I went around the crowded noisy hall, a teenage girl who was gently feeding a young boy caught my attention. She must be his elder sister, I thought to myself. I approached them and asked where their mother was. She was looking for a job that day, I was told. So she sent her teenage daughter to feed the boy. Thinking that she must be as hungry as her brother, I asked, "Have you eaten?" "No," she said, "I am not part of the program. I am already thirteen." I was surprised at her honesty. For hungry children, this was an opportunity to cheat in order to fill one's stomach. But she remained honest. I responded, "I will instruct a volunteer to give you lunch, if some food is left after all the children have eaten." Thankful but embarrassed, she said, "No, bishop. There are many other hungry children in this village. Give the extra food to them." I was drawn into deep silence. "My God, my God, why are these children going hungry?" I prayed. Yet I also exclaimed, "I did not expect to see sharing and integrity in this place of death. Truly these are innocent children of God. There is hope for the world."

In eucharistic adoration, let us join the centurion in watching over Jesus and see what he has seen. Let us cringe in horror at the sight of destructive evil. Let us marvel at the reality of spotless love, of pure sacrifice and worship. I wish that eucharistic adoration would lead us to know Jesus more as the compassionate companion of many crucified peoples of today. Let us spend time too with the multitudes of innocent victims of our time. We might be able to touch Jesus who knows their tears and pain, for he has made them his own and has changed them into hope and love. Watching over our suffering neighbors, we could be changed, like the centurion, into discerners of truth and heralds of faith. And hopefully when people behold how we bear others' crosses in love, they too would see the face of innocence and the Son of

God in us. Let us adore Jesus, who offered his life as a gift to the Father for us sinners. Let us adore him for ourselves, for the poor, for the earth, for the church, and for the life of the world.

—delivered on June 19, 2008, at
the 49th International Eucharistic
Congress in Quebec City, Canada

Telling the Story of Jesus
Mission in Asia

The Asian Mission Congress is an occasion to celebrate the calling of the church to be missionary. It recalls with gratitude the missionary paths the church has already taken in Asia. It rejoices at the continuing efforts at mission, with testimonies of valor, faith, and love. It invites us to commit ourselves once again to the perennial bidding of Jesus Christ that we bring the good news of the reign of God to all the earth. It urges us to seek new ways of understanding and doing mission, faithful to the church's rich tradition but responsive to the realities faced by the peoples of Asia.

It can be said that the history of the church is the history of mission. This multilayered and multicolored history, dating from New Testament times, testifies to the many ways by which the church has understood and practiced mission. We can add the fact that while the one church is universal, it exists in local churches that have quite unique histories and situations, and therefore quite unique experiences and notions of mission. Pope John Paul II affirms in *Redemptoris Missio* (RM) a basic insight of *Ad Gentes* (AG) that mission, a single but complex reality, is developed in a variety of ways.[1] In continuity with the church's dynamic search for ways of doing mission appropriate to specific times and places our congress proposes an understanding and practice of mission focused on the story of Jesus in Asia.

A story is never just a story. A story is truly a story when told or narrated, and hopefully listened to. Nowadays, one of the names of storytelling is sharing. In *Ecclesia in Asia* (EAs), John Paul II describes mission as sharing the light of faith in Jesus, a gift received and a gift to be shared with the peoples of Asia.[2] That sharing can take the form of telling the story of Jesus. I believe that storytelling provides a creative framework for understanding mission in Asia, a continent whose cultures and religions are rooted in great stories or epics. John Paul II also recognizes the narrative methods akin to Asian cultural forms as a preferred way of proclaiming Jesus in Asia (EAs 20).

Understanding "Story" and Telling Story

Human life is unimaginable without stories. Life itself has a narrative structure. Story mediates life and its meaning. Telling stories comes so naturally to us that we do not reflect sufficiently on its significance for our lives. In recent years, scholars have been rediscovering the role of narrative in their respective disciplines. Theology and spirituality have benefited from this "turn to the story."[3] Mission can equally be enriched. Let us devote some time to reflect on story and storytelling. My presentation will be far from exhaustive. As an invitation to further reflection and discussion, this paper will dwell only on those aspects that might have a bearing on understanding mission as telling the story of Jesus.

1. Good stories are based on experience. There are good stories and bad ones. But the difference does not always depend on the style of the narrator or the ending of the story. Ultimately we want a credible story, a story that is believable because it is true. The strongest basis of truth is the firsthand experience of the narrator. While credible reporters of somebody else's experience can be believed in, nothing matches the story of someone who actually was there when an incident happened, for the event is now a part of the person. We tell our best stories when they are about our experience. Our best stories are about who we are.

2. Stories reveal personal identity and people and events that shaped that identity. Stories reveal who we are, the flow and sense of our lives and where we are going. My story is my autobiography, my identity in the great scheme of things.[4] As I tell my little stories, my fundamental life story is revealed not only to the listener but also and primarily to me, the narrator. I make sense of myself. But I realize in the process that the story is not simply about me. It is also always about other people, my family and friends, society, culture, the economy, or what we call "the times." My story is not developed in a vacuum. I am what I am because I am immersed in other people's stories and the stories of my time. If I neglect or deny them, I have no personal story to tell. In telling my story, I make sense also of the world I inhabit.

3. Stories are dynamic, open to reinterpretation and retelling, and transformative. Personal identity is shaped by interaction with the world put into memory. Remembrance is vital if we want to grow in self-knowledge. But we remember by telling stories.[5]

Memory is made of stories rather than mere chronology, and stories bring experience back to mind.[6] By remembering, we realize that the past is not at all static. It continues to mold us. It can also be seen in a new light from the optic provided by new experiences. In fact, we tell the same story in different fashions. Stories reveal what made us what we are now while differentiating us from what we were before and opening possibilities for the future. Through stories we get in touch with the dynamism of transformation of personal identity: how much we have changed and how much more we have to change.

4. *Stories are the ground for understanding spiritual, doctrinal, and ethical symbols.* Stories disclose personal identity by surfacing the values, moral norms, and priorities of a person. The spirituality of a person emerges in his or her story. Ethical, spiritual, and doctrinal symbols precious to a person are derived from that person's life stories. Those profound living symbols are understood only when the story is known and heard.[7] Stories are indispensable to the meaning of a person's faith and moral symbols.

5. *Stories form community.* What we have said so far about story and personal identity is also true of

the identity of a community. Common experience and memories bind unique individuals into a cohesive body. The narrative privileged by a community becomes the nucleus of its values, ethics, and spirituality.[8] A community's distinguishing beliefs, rituals, celebrations, customs, and lifestyle will make sense to us only if we go back to the stories that the members of that community hold and cherish in common.

6. Stories when received can transform the listener. Important experiences are named and told in stories.[9] When we experience something positively or negatively significant, we cannot wait to tell it to someone. This dynamic tells us that story begs for a listener, for someone with whom to share. One's story can awaken memories of similar experiences in a listener, open new meanings, create wonder, and shake from slumber. The engagement and response from the listener begin when the narrator concludes.[10] The narrator's story is woven with the listener's story to produce new stories. Usually a good listener will become a good storyteller. The one who has experienced weaving another person's stories into one's own by listening will be secure enough to share one's story as a thread in someone else's story.

7. Stories can be told in a variety of ways. A story can be told in many ways, even when not literally telling a story. Oral narration is still the most common. But stories can be told through writing letters, novels, or poems. Photographs and video productions are technologically inspired ways of telling stories. A person's gestures, mannerisms, tone of voice, facial contortions, and body postures are as present as any character in a story. A person's silence can be a powerful way of telling a story. By extension, a person's attitudes, lifestyle, and relationships tell stories and generate new stories. A community's dances, music, art, architecture, and food are essential elements of its story. Stories are so richly textured that they are open to many ways of being narrated.

8. Stories can be suppressed. Even if telling stories comes spontaneously to us, some factors can suppress storytelling. The pain brought about by a traumatic memory, shame, or guilt can prevent a victim from telling his or her full story. In order to preserve a bit of dignity after a harrowing experience, a victim can deny that a story is part of his or her personal identity and memory. Dictators forbid stories of corruption, oppression, killings, and destruction from being told, lest their regime be put into jeopardy. They bribe media people and threaten those who want to expose the truth. They impose an official national history that erases memories that would put them in a bad light. Some stories are too dangerous to tell, for listeners might hear the call for transformation. The fiercest battles being waged daily are over stories. But healing is possible. Where victims are allowed to tell their stories to friends, counselors, or professionals who show compassion and understanding, their self-worth slowly comes back. Where communities reclaim their true story, they reclaim too their power for societal change.

We spent time reflecting on story and storytelling to uncover their potential for the understanding and practice of mission.

Mission as Telling the Story of Jesus in Asia

At the outset, we affirm with *Ad Gentes* of Vatican II that the pilgrim church is missionary by nature because it takes its origin from the mission of Jesus Christ and the mission of the Holy Spirit in accordance with the saving will of the Father (AG 2). So that what Jesus has accomplished for the salvation of all may come in time to achieve its effect in all, he sent the Holy Spirit from the Father to carry out his saving work inwardly and in the church (AG 3–4). It is therefore fitting to call the Holy Spirit the principal agent of mission, as Pope John Paul II does (cf. RM, chap. III). It is the Holy Spirit that enables the church to accomplish the mission entrusted to it (EAs 43).

From this perspective, the missions of Jesus Christ and the Holy Spirit can be considered God's own story. God is the "teller of the tale."[11] The Holy Spirit will tell the story of Jesus to the church. Jesus promised, "the [Counselor], the Holy Spirit, whom the Father will send in my name, will teach you everything, and remind you of all that I have said to you" (John 14:26). The three persons of the Trinity are even depicted by Jesus as "telling stories" to one another. "When the Spirit of truth comes, he will guide you into all the truth; for he will not speak on his own, but will speak whatever he hears. . . . He will glorify me, because he will take what is mine and declare it to you. All that the Father has is mine. For this reason I said that he will take what is mine and declare it to you" (John 16:13-15). The church's mission is a fruit of the story that the Holy Spirit declares to it from Jesus and the Father. The origin of the church's mission is the great storyteller, the Holy Spirit, to whom it must listen so it can share what it has heard. The church is God's storyteller of Jesus Christ as it listens to the Holy Spirit.

That the church should tell the story of Jesus goes without saying. The great question for Asia is *how* to share the story, as John Paul II accurately points out (EAs 19). The "how" aspect of the mission has been the concern of many Asian theologians, like Michael Amaladoss, SJ.[12] Using some of our reflections on the understanding of story, let us look at mission as telling the story of Jesus under the guidance of the Holy Spirit.

1. The church tells the story of Jesus from its experience of Jesus. Telling the story of Jesus in Asia is more effective if it springs from the experience of the storyteller. Pope Paul VI's observation in *Evangelii Nuntiandi* that people today put more trust in witnesses than in teachers is universally true but more so in Asia where cultures put particular emphasis on the experientially verified truthfulness of the witness.[13] The earliest apostles, who were Asians, spoke of their experience—what they have heard, seen with their eyes, looked upon, and touched with their hands concerning the Word of life (1 John 1:1-4). There cannot be any other way for the contemporary church in Asia. Without a deep experience of Jesus as Savior, how can I tell his story convincingly as part of my personal story? The experience of St. Paul is truly the root of mission when he says, "it is no longer I who live, but it is Christ who lives in me. And the life I now live in the flesh I live by faith in the Son of God, who loved me and gave himself for me" (Gal 2:20). Telling the story of Jesus in Asia requires the church's living encounter with Jesus in prayer, worship, interaction with people, especially the poor, and events that constitute the "signs of the times."

2. The story of Jesus manifests the identity of the church among the poor, cultures, and religions of Asia. Just as a story reveals personal identity, a story of faith in Jesus reveals also the identity of the narrator as a believer. A witness who tells one's story of encountering Jesus cannot and should not hide one's identity as a disciple of the Savior. But just as a web of relationships with people, cultures, and societal currents form a personal story or identity, so is Christian storytelling in Asia to be done in relationship with others. The Christian identity and story in Asia is always with and not apart from those of other cultures and religions. The story of Jesus is to be told by Asian Christians who are with and among the poor, the diverse cultures, and the various religions of Asia that partly determine their identities and stories as Asians. This reality of Asia has prompted Jonathan Yun-Ka Tan to propose that *missio ad* (toward) *gentes* should be understood now according to the new paradigm of *missio inter* (among or with) *gentes*.[14] But I hold that *missio ad gentes* should not be eliminated but should rather be done *inter gentes*. There can never be a genuine mission *toward* people without it being at the same time mission *with* people. And genuine mission *with* people encourages mission *toward* people. With and among the poor, cultures, and religions, Asian Christians are *Asian*. To and for the poor, cultures, and religions, Asian Christians are *Christian*. The blending of these stories, I believe, can enrich the numerous reflections of the Federation of Asian Bishops' Conferences (FABC) on mission as dialogue with the poor, cultures, and religions of Asia.[15]

3. The church keeps the memory of Jesus dynamically alive. Among and for other Asians, the church tells the story of Jesus in the mode of keeping the memory of Jesus alive. Keeping the memory of Jesus does not mean locking it up in some untouchable realm of existence. It is kept when reappropriated and shared. Trusting in the Holy Spirit and faithful to the memory guaranteed in the tradition of the universal church, the church in Asia should have the courage to redis-cover new ways of telling the story of Jesus, retrieving its vitality and freeing its potential for the renewal of the Asian realities. The story of Jesus, when guarded as a museum piece, fails to be life-giving. In *Ecclesia in Asia* (EAs 19–20, 22) John Paul II poses the chal-lenge of finding the pedagogy that would make the story of Jesus closer to Asian sensibilities, especially to theologians. He is confident that the same story could be told in new perspectives and in the light of new circumstances.

4. *The story of Jesus provides meaning to the church's symbols of faith.* We said that stories contain the mean-ing of the spirituality, ethics, and convictions em-braced by a person. It can happen that the church can be so identified with some "standardized" or stereo-typed symbols of doctrine, ethics, and worship that the story that gives impetus to them is forgotten. Then the symbols themselves lose their power to touch people. The symbols of faith must be rooted back to the foundational story of Jesus. For example,

the breaking of bread at the Eucharist should be seen in many stories of sharing, caring, and communion, without which the ritual is deprived of significance. A bishop's ring should spring from a living story of service to the community, without which the ring is reduced to a piece of jewelry. A priest's symbolism as Jesus' presence should spring from a living story of availability to people, without which the priesthood becomes a status rather than a vocation. The symbols of faith must be traceable to the foundational story of Jesus. A return to the story of Jesus would also enable the church in Asia to correct the impressions of foreignness attached to its doctrine, rituals, and symbols (EAs 20). Detached from the originating story of Jesus, the symbols of the church might tell of a story foreign to Jesus himself.

5. The story of Jesus generates the church. Stories also form a community, as we have already stated. In common experience and memory communities find cohesion and common value. The common memory of the story of Jesus generated by the Holy Spirit should be the fundamental source of unity and identity in faith of the church in Asia. The Scriptures, the sacraments, especially the Eucharist, the doctrines, the rituals, and the whole tradition are ways of constantly telling the story of Jesus so as to keep his memory the core of the Christian community. But this sense of community is not an excuse to isolate the church so that it could preserve its identity. The story of Jesus that makes it a Christian community is the same story that the whole community must share. In the paradigm of storytelling, the church loses its identity if it fails to tell the story that is its very identity. "For those who want to save their life will lose it, and those who lose their life for my sake, and for the sake of the gospel, will save it," Jesus says (Mark 8:35). It has been the conviction of the FABC that it is the whole church that is called to mission.[16] The local churches need to discern and develop the many gifts inspired by the Holy Spirit so that they could contribute to the telling of Jesus' story. The whole church, the fruit of the story of Jesus, becomes its narrator.

6. A listening church tells the story of Jesus. Stories find their completion in the listener. But stories that are imposed are not listened to. The church in Asia must trust in the vitality of the story it offers, without any thought of forcing it on others. It is already a beautiful story that will surely touch those who have even a bit of openness. John Paul II tells us in *Ecclesia in Asia* that we share the gift of Jesus not to proselytize but out of obedience to the Lord and as an act of service to the peoples of Asia (EAs 20). Let the story speak and touch. Let the Holy Spirit open the hearts and memories of the listeners and invite them to transformation. The multitudes of poor peoples of Asia can find compassion and hope in Jesus' story. The cultures of Asia will resonate with the disturbing challenge to true freedom in Jesus' story. The various religions of Asia will marvel at the respect and appreciation toward those seeking God and genuine holiness in Jesus' story. The church in Asia is called to humbly allow the Spirit to touch its listeners. As a storyteller of the Holy Spirit, the church in Asia is to enter the worlds and languages of its listeners and from within them to tell Jesus' story just like at Pentecost.[17] But that means the church in Asia must be a good listener to the Spirit and to the poor, cultures, and religions if it is to speak meaningfully at all. A storytelling church must be a listening church.[18]

7. *The church tells the story of Jesus in a multiplicity of ways.* Stories can be told in a variety of ways. So can the story of Jesus. The church in Asia, with its rich

heritage of storytelling acquired from Asian homes, neighborhoods, religions, and traditional wisdoms, can be creative in telling the story of Jesus. The witness of a holy, ethical, and upright life is still the best story about Jesus in Asia.[19] The lives of holy men and women and martyrs show how the story of Jesus is inscribed in persons and communities.[20] Men and women who have dedicated themselves to service of neighbor, like Blessed Teresa of Calcutta, are living stories that Asian peoples love to hear. Defense of the poor, work for justice, promotion of life, caring for the sick, educating children and the youth, peacemaking, alleviation of foreign debt, and stewardship of creation are some ways of retelling Jesus' story in Asia today.[21] But the church must also be ready to accept the Holy Spirit's surprising ways of retelling the story of Jesus.

8. *The church is the voice of suppressed stories.* It is a scandal that suppression of stories is a daily occurrence in many parts of Asia. The poor, the girl-child, women, refugees, migrants, the minorities, the indigenous peoples, the victims of different types of domestic, political, ethnic violence, and the environment are but a few of those whose stories are suppressed. Many are afraid of the stories they will tell. Or are they afraid

to hear the truth and its demands? The church tells the story of Jesus, whose words often fell on deaf ears and who was executed so that he could be prevented from telling his story. So in Asia the church pays tribute to him by allowing itself to be the storyteller of the voiceless so that Jesus' voice may be heard in their suppressed stories.

Conclusion

Mission as telling of the story of Jesus is already taking place in Asia. We celebrate the many storytellers of the Holy Spirit whose stories, though hidden, have generated new stories in the lives of many Asian brothers and sisters.

I close by turning to Jesus, the Logos or story of God and master storyteller of the reign of God. Let us behold him. Let us listen to him. Let us learn from him. Let us open ourselves to his story and his storytelling. His story is about the Abba he has experienced and the fullness of life Abba offers. His life and identity were rooted in this constant union with Abba. Yet he lived like an ordinary Jew, an ordinary Asian, with family, friends, women, children, foreigners, temple officials, the teachers of the law, the poor, the sick, the friendless, the sinners and enemies. They were all part of who he was. He gathered a community, a new family of those who would listen to God's word and act on it. He told them stories of Abba and life in Abba. He used their language. His parables were simple yet disarming. He told them about Abba through his meals, healing, compassion, mercy, forgiveness, and critique of false religiosity. His story leads him to a supper where he was food and where he washed the feet of his friends. Nothing could stop him from telling his story, even on the cross. His humiliating death should have been the end of his story. But Abba had something more to say: "My Son—he is truly risen." Pouring his gift of the Holy Spirit into our hearts, Jesus entrusts his story to us. I hear him saying, "Listen to my story. Go and tell my story again and again where it all began—in my home, in my beloved Asia!"

—delivered on October 19, 2006,
at the Asian Mission Congress in
Chiang Mai, Thailand

Notes

1. Second Vatican Council, Decree on the Missionary Activity of the Church (*Ad Gentes*), December 7, 1965, no. 6; John Paul II, Encyclical Letter on the Permanent Validity of the Church's Missionary Mandate (*Redemptoris Missio*), July 12, 1990, no. 41.

2. Saint John Paul II, Post-Synodal Apostolic Exhortation on Jesus Christ the Saviour and His Mission of Love and Service in Asia (*Ecclesia in Asia*), June 11, 1999, no. 10.

3. An example among many is Michael L. Cook, SJ, *Christology as Narrative Quest* (Collegeville, MN: Liturgical Press, 1997).

4. Richard Woods, OP, "Good News: The Story Teller as Evangelist," *New Blackfriars* 81 (2000): 206.

5. Ibid., 205.

6. Richard Bayuk, CPPS, "Preaching and the Imagination," *The Bible Today* 38 (2000): 289, 292.

7. Cook, *Christology as Narrative Quest*, 31.

8. Jose Mario C. Francisco, SJ, "The Mediating Role of Narrative in Inter-Religious Dialogue: Implications and Illustrations from the Philippine Context," *East Asian Pastoral Review* 41 (2004): 164.

9. Bayuk, "Preaching and the Imagination," 289.

10. Ibid., 290.

11. Cook, *Christology as Narrative Quest*, 39.

12. See the following works of Michael Amaladoss, SJ, "Images of Jesus in India," *East Asian Pastoral Review* 31 (1994): 6–20; and "'Who Do You Say that I Am?' Speaking of Jesus in India Today," *East Asian Pastoral Review* 34 (1997): 211–24.

13. Blessed Pope Paul VI, Apostolic Exhortation on Evangelization in the Modern World (*Evangelii Nuntiandi*), December 8, 1975, no. 41.

14. Jonathan Yun-Ka Tan, *Missio Inter Gentes: Towards a New Paradigm in the Mission Theology of the FABC*, FABC Papers No. 109.

15. The fundamental document is FABC I (1974), "Evangelization in Modern Day Asia," especially nos. 12, 14, 20, G. Rosales and C. G. Arevalo, eds., *For All the Peoples of Asia*, vol. I (Quezon City: Claretian, 1997), 11–25. Many plenary assemblies and institutes of the FABC are further elucidations of the basic insight of FABC I in changing circumstances.

16. See BIMA III (Third Bishops' Institute for Missionary Apostolate, 1982), no. 5; Ibid., 104.

17. BIRA IV/12 (Twelfth Bishops' Institute for Interreligious Affairs on the Theology of Dialogue, 1991), nos. 42–47; Ibid., 332.

18. BIRA I (First Bishops' Institute for Interreligious Affairs, 1979), nos. 11–14; Ibid., 111.

19. BIMA III (Third Bishops' Institute for Missionary Apostolate, 1982), no. 10; Ibid., 105.

20. Francisco, "The Mediating Role of Narrative," 167.

21. EAs 33–41.